Love

and

Little Birds

Love

and

Little Birds

*Wrestling with the
Sadness of Dementia*

J OHN R ADWAY

ARCHWAY
PUBLISHING

Archway Publishing books may be ordered through booksellers or by contacting:

Archway Publishing
1663 Liberty Drive
Bloomington, IN 47403
www.archwaypublishing.com
1-(888)-242-5904

ISBN: 978-1-4808-0095-3 (sc)
ISBN: 978-1-4808-0096-0 (e)

Library of Congress Control Number: 2013908937

Printed in the United States of America

Archway Publishing rev. date: 5/15/2013

Cover photo by Linda Mestek
www.capturingthewest.com

Contents

Introduction

We all know that the human brain is desperately fragile in some ways and incredibly powerful in many others. Dementia is the quintessential example of mental fragility, but dealing with dementia can awaken the full power of the brain in those who are obliged to care for its victims. This little book is the fusion of two "diaries" I have been writing in my attempts to come to grips with my own loss—the death from dementia of the love of my life almost three years ago. I started these diaries soon after I had committed her to the loving care of a facility specializing in dementia. There had been no time at all for writing in the final two years of my caregiving. The first section describes my attempts to grasp the meaning of dementia, and the second is a very personal chronicle of my tortuous journey through the ruins of my previous life into a new one.

It is not a terminally sad journey, and it's not over yet. I have been helped along the way by good friends and by the staff of the hospice organization that took care of my wife in the end, especially through my participation in the support group they offer. The experience of dementia caregiving is unique and not fully comprehensible to those who have not lived it. A good support group can create a stunning bond between its members, springing from an awareness of the universality of human suffering and the fact that it can be overcome only by the power of universal compassion and love. It seems quite ironic that dealing with dementia, a disease that destroys the mind, can lead to such a hopeful conclusion. But I firmly believe that the vicissitudes of life are never so harsh and cruel that they cannot be borne and eventually reduced through those immediately accessible and understandable emotions of compassion and love. I have a hunch that we need not look too much further than that to discover the meaning of life itself. And that is what this book is all about.

PART I

Shape and Shadow, Form and Function:
The Structure of Progressive Dementia

I married my wife, Claire, on Thanksgiving Day, 1961, after a very short courtship—we had made up our minds in a hurry, and we never regretted our decision. She was a schoolteacher then, but she had to give up her career within a year after our marriage because of a seizure disorder. The seizures she suffered did not disrupt our married life in any significant way. In fact, they enhanced it, because I was induced by her disorder to give up my career as a prosecutor and become a farmer so that I could be closer to her in case she needed my assistance. And we became very close: inseparable, in fact, which made the eventual onset of her dementia in 2003 especially devastating. We had become one, and her dementia tore us apart.

The assertion that the slow but inexorable passage into dementia of one's lifelong love, partner, friend, and trusted advisor is tragic is a huge understatement. The reality is almost impossible to describe. That being the case, I have been looking for a way to describe the process itself, to give the evolution of the degeneration a shape that I can grasp. Even though I have an undergraduate degree in philosophy and have become somewhat familiar with current ideas concerning the structure of the brain and the nature of thought—cognitive science and neurology, philosophy of mind, artificial intelligence, and the like—my familiarity with them is superficial. I do not to pretend to fully understand them, and I have, to a large extent, simplified the ideas I draw from them. I am only trying to organize my own perceptions of dementia into a form, or forms, that I can understand. I am going to call those forms *realities*.

Boxes and What They Contain:
The Shape of Reality

I had just returned one afternoon from the care facility in which my wife, Claire, was living, when it struck me that realities can be viewed as a series of boxes—not ordered by the quality of each reality, not rated one better than another, but just a series of boxes running into infinity. You and I operate each within our own box; it may be almost the same box for each, or it may be different in a good many ways. Each box is filled according to our backgrounds, our memories, our education, our beliefs, our ethnicity, and our position in society. When the brain begins to deteriorate, one enters other boxes, other kinds of reality: at first very similar to the box one has occupied before and then increasingly different as the dementia progresses. Claire, for instance, had moved from her original box into maybe three or four others since the process of deterioration began. In each box, she had functioned according to the reality contained therein, and there were processes of logic that made perfect sense to her within each box.

That afternoon, an older lady cradling her "baby," a very realistic doll, approached me, smiled, picked up my forearm, and exclaimed, "No, that's too heavy!" She smiled again and sat down across the room with her institutional friend, who gently reminded her that "Perhaps now the baby should sleep." All this was perfectly normal to her; she was operating flawlessly within the box she then occupied. It may not be the box I occupy, but the logic that guides our thinking was the same, even though her box, her reality, was very different from mine, just as mine and hers were different from the box that Claire occupied then.

Now, when we think of reality, we don't particularly like to think of ourselves as being in boxes. But when we agree that reality for a Buddhist monk in Japan is very different from reality for an average American in, say, Phoenix, Arizona, we are perhaps acknowledging that realities can be different even for people operating without dementia.

What about science? you say. Surely science probes and articulates realities that are indisputably "right," that are eternal and not contained in any box but can be relied on as actual "true" realities in every sense. Let's take as an example the perception of the reality of the universe at the beginning of the twentieth century. In 1900, there were no fully formed concepts of galaxies; the universe consisted of a whole lot of stars and imperfectly understood nebulae—vague, bright shapes in the far reaches of the visible universe. Everything seemed very stable; even Albert Einstein subscribed to the theory of a "steady-state" universe at one time.

Then, in 1912, astronomer V. M. Slipher, of Lowell Observatory in Flagstaff, Arizona, measured the spectra of the light from some of these nebulae and discovered that these spectra were shifted to the red, which meant that the objects were moving away from us. I think that it was Slipher, or one of his contemporaries, who first called these objects "galaxies." In the 1920s, astronomer Edwin Hubble, at the Mount Wilson Observatory near Los Angeles, found that the further away from us the galaxies were, the greater was their redshift, which meant that distant galaxies were moving away from us faster than nearer ones. From this finding, the Big Bang theory was derived, which posits that the universe began as a point that suddenly exploded, creating matter and energy, which rapidly expanded in, or with, time and space. This expansion continues to this day and is in fact accelerating. And to this day, there continues an argument about whether the universe will continue to expand forever, to reach a steady state eventually, or collapse at last and return to a point—perhaps to expand again in another big bang.

Nor is that the only uncertainty. A large number of scientists have postulated quite recently that the stars and galaxies and other objects we can see in the universe account for only a small amount of the mass and energy that must be present to explain its continuing expansion and that there may be an enormous amount of "dark matter" and "dark energy" present in the universe that we know nothing about. Most recently, some bold astronomers are wondering whether the universe is expanding not in space but in three-dimensional time as quantum phenomena, which would solve the mystery of "dark energy."

Are these realities—as revealed by science, which involves the construction and careful testing of hypotheses by observation and experimentation—indisputable and eternal? No, they are not; the hypotheses and the data that support them are constantly changing and expanding, and even the most honest scientists can disagree on these realities and change them with more hypotheses and data. In short, scientists are creating perceptions of reality that fit with other perceptions into each of our reality boxes, and like these other perceptions, scientific ones are mutable and imperfect and subject to many different interpretations.

Layers within the Boxes:
Changing Shapes

The brain is composed of layers within layers: layers of neurons, layers of connections, layers of circuits, layers of function; it is the destruction, the peeling away of those layers, from whatever cause, that results in dementia. At first, the comprehension of reality is altered only a little; there are little lapses of memory and losses of minor skills, hardly noticed by victim or observer. But then it accelerates; the splendid sunset becomes the harbinger of terrifying night, the smile of reassurance by the caregiver becomes a menacing grimace, and the plastic doll becomes the beloved baby. Why does reality change for the victim in this fashion? The brain is an incredibly complex mechanism. It contains a hundred billion neurons and trillions of synapses, the connections between neurons, all organized into circuits or "modules." These collect the data from sensory organs, transmit them to cognitive areas within the brain, and then process them into consciousness and cognition, control movements and emotions, and literally coordinate and control all the processes within our bodies.

These modules are interconnected in extremely complex ways. The input from the eyes, for instance, passes through a good many of the modules before being transformed into vision, and if certain visual modules in an individual's brain are not functioning, that individual is sometimes able to "see" without being conscious of seeing—is able to walk, pick up objects, and generally function normally, while asserting "I am blind." The robots that assemble automobiles in factories operate in just the same way. Their sensors guide their movements, but the robots cannot be said to "see" things, to have an awareness of what they are looking at in any way similar to the way vision brings awareness to a normally functioning human being.

Thus the idea of dementia begins to take shape. The two most important products of brain activity are awareness, or consciousness, and action. Any deterioration of the mechanisms that produce these, the neurons and the modules and their interconnections, has a profound effect on cognition—which is, in a way, the sum of awareness and action, by which I mean *interaction*, with the external world. Therefore, the person who acts as though she were sighted while thinking that she is blind is, in a very real sense, actually blind, because that is the reality of which she is aware, the box in which she is living. For us as human beings, reality, the reality in which we operate, is what we *think* it is, because it is the only reality of which we are *aware*. And the mechanisms that produce the state of dementia are the same ones that produce that state of blindness, that is, the deterioration of the neurons and modules and connections that produce our awareness of reality.

Dealing with Dementia:
The Shadow of Reality

So how do these ideas about brain structure and function affect those of us whose painful duty it is to care for a friend or family member for whom the shape of reality is changing almost every day? The main idea we need to focus on is just that change. We need to be aware that the change is enormously complex, driven not only by the deterioration of neurons and modules and connections but by the underlying plasticity of the brain, often not completely destroyed by the dementia until the end. New connections are constantly being made in the brain in an attempt to bypass the injuries caused by the deteriorations that fuel the dementia.

We need to remember always that the victim of dementia has not—absolutely not—entered a state of "second childhood"; that term has been used since time immemorial, but it does not reflect the reality of adult dementia. The dementia patient is in possession not of a child's brain but of a completely developed adult brain that has been damaged by her dementia.

Thus, toward the end, my wife, Claire, had mercurial twists of realities. She woke often during the night; on one awakening she would scream at me, "Who are you? What are you doing in my house? Get out!" and on the very next awakening, maybe an hour or two later, she would greet me with a hug, and say, "Oh, John, thank God you're here."

Just days before I reluctantly placed my wife in a memory-care facility, this gentle lady—who could no longer dress herself and sometimes violently resisted my assistance and who required my help with the simplest aspects of everyday living—sat down with me on the couch and patiently, intelligently, and compassionately explained that something was terribly wrong with her brain and that I should take her to a place where she could be cared for because I looked so tired.

The caregiver must be sensitive to these changes, must humor the victim when she is deluded, but must never be condescending or abrupt. And he must always remember, as well, that it is the nature of dementia to worsen over time and that the time will come when it will be impossible for him to care for his loved one. And he must be aware that the decision to institutionalize her will be by far the most difficult one he has made in his life. Let me make myself brutally clear here: you must rely on your doctor, your family, and your friends to tell you when it is time for a care facility to take over your task. I delayed until it was almost too late, and I know of cases where the caregiver procrastinated until it *was* too late. And most importantly of all, you must accept the fact that placing your beloved in a caring and competent facility when you can no longer safely care for her yourself is the ultimate expression of your love for her.

Dealing with Death:

The Cruelest Reality

The death of a loved one, particularly a beloved spouse whom one has cherished for many decades, is always devastating. But when that death is preceded by dementia, the survivor is left physically debilitated and mentally and emotionally drained in a particularly poignant way and is suddenly thrust into a completely altered reality. So what's it like to live in that reality? It's different for everyone, to be sure, but for me, it seemed as though our life was a house that had been consumed by a fire, and there I was, squatting in the ashes, poking at the sad, burnt remains of what had been our precious possessions and searching for anything that might give me a clue to the reality of what our house may have been, of what our life may have meant.

Now, does that differ in any significant way from the loss suffered from a death not preceded by dementia or any other form of long-term wasting disease? Yes, it does; it's a dramatically different experience. My now-lost wife and I had discussed it often during our lives, because our parents had experienced it, and we had experienced it with them. In each case, one parent had died after a lingering dementia, and the other parent had not. In each case, we were able to immediately grieve, and deal with our grief, for the parent who had died from pneumonia or a sudden heart attack, but it took us a long time to even remember who the parent who had been slowly felled by dementia had been before his affliction, which led to feelings of guilt in us, the survivors.

Why was that? It was not that the parent who had been afflicted with dementia was less loved—quite the contrary. It was, rather, that our grieving process for the dementia victims had begun when the reality of the result became apparent to us, when we became fully aware that we had already, in a very real way, lost that parent or spouse. And so, death in those cases was a sort of anticlimax, not a shock. Thus the grieving was less intense, and for that arose the feelings of guilt.

How did we deal with that guilt? My mother and my wife, both of whom often had piercing insights into human nature, began by getting out old photo albums, looking at pictures of the parents who had been afflicted with dementia, and finding and reading letters they had written. The photos and letters inspired memories of those parents before their afflictions had become severe. After a while, we realized that we had felt their loss long before they'd died, and the guilt arising from our tepid grieving at the time of their actual deaths was greatly diminished.

That is why I am now sifting through the ashes of the wonderful life I shared with my friend and companion of almost half a century. I have found our own old photographs and letters and talked with old mutual friends about their memories, and I am remembering my wife and me as we used to be. My guilt is rapidly disappearing, and I am beginning to achieve a sort of acceptance of my tremendous loss.

After the Ashes Have Cooled:
Rebuilding Reality

Here is a poem I wrote in June 2011 on the anniversary of my wife's death.

> Summer Breeze
> Were we a pair? Weren't we just!
> At first two drifting wisps of dust
> whisked together by a summer breeze,
> then wafted up with breathless ease
> to the tallest mountain tops above,
> by the lasting fullness of our love.

According to all that I have heard and read, and now from my own experience, I've learned that grieving for a lost loved one is a complex and lengthy process—and a highly individual one, as well. I should note in that regard that Claire and I had neither siblings nor children, and consequently I was deprived of a certain amount of support during the course of my struggle with dementia and bereavement; but on the other hand, I suffered none of the complications which stem from sometimes misinformed family attempts to help. I attended for a while the meetings of a grief support group, and I was not really surprised to discover that some of my fellow attendees had been going to those meetings of as long as three or four years.

I can relate to that; I don't think I shall ever fully recover. But there is a fine line between grief and self-pity, and I feel that the time has come for me to look forward instead of back. How does one go about doing that? It involves building a whole new reality, based in large part upon prior realities, but striking out into new territories too—not easy for me after all those years of an extremely close and happy marriage, a marriage which completely filled my old reality.

There is just one more lingering effect of caregiving that I must mention before moving on to the future. I can't say this enough: the dementia care-giving experience leaves the caregiver completely drained, physically and emotionally, and the recovery process can be long and tedious. Underlying medical problems—mine was a cardiac arrhythmia—can become serious as a result and, together with all the other lingering effects of prolonged exhaustion, can lead to a potentially disabling loss of confidence in one's ability to cope with life's challenges. I have been afflicted with this problem in good measure. The fear that I am no longer capable of dealing with complex activities—like traveling, for instance—has almost stopped me from doing so on several occasions. I have also noted this problem in a number of my fellow sufferers, mostly men, but women are also susceptible.

So what causes this loss of confidence? Dealing with dementia is, more than anything else, extremely frustrating, both for the victim and the caregiver. The victim is frustrated that she can no longer care for herself or deal with her altered realities in any meaningful way, and the caregiver is frustrated because nothing he does seems to make any improvement at all in the situation—in fact, things always do get worse as the disease progresses, no matter what he does. After a while, these frustrations come to define what is normal, and the caregiver becomes convinced that he is unable to successfully execute any complex task. This way of thinking is a habit that is far from trivial; it is not in the least easy to break, but it must be overcome if life is to continue to be meaningful.

There are many ways to deal with this problem, but I have found that the only one that works for me is the most direct. If I really want to do something, I simply force myself to plan for it. Then, when the time comes to do, it I tell myself that I will be stronger for doing it but will absolutely never forgive myself if I renege. I am, indeed, regaining some of my self confidence; I have not yet reneged. It's not easy, but failure is not an option. Helplessness does breed hopelessness, and what is life without hope?

Now this section of the book begins with a poem, and you may well wonder why writing poetry is relevant to the on-going rebuilding of reality for a bereaved dementia caregiver. The act of writing down our passing thoughts, in any form, gives them substance and structure. I am giving a shape to my own thoughts, at this instant, as I write them down here. They exist here on the paper, to be examined and reexamined, to be woven into the new reality I must construct for myself, like a house, in which I will live the rest of my life. The poems speak to the emotions; I can write them only when I am deeply moved by something, and I am reminded when I reread them that my feelings about our marriage, and the strength that I have always derived from it, must always be major parts of my ongoing realities.

My wife was dyslexic, and she learned to read with the help of her very kind and patient parents and teachers. Perhaps as a result of her early experiences, she became a very eager reader, especially of history and English literature. After her graduation from college she became a very effective reading teacher of first and second graders. Her curiosity never abated, and it was infectious. We delighted in learning things together; I am carrying on that tradition with enthusiasm. And I am at least partly helping myself to accept my loss of Claire by telling myself that I am doing these things because of her, and in a small way, I am sharing them with her now.

The Shape of the Future:
Banishing the Shadows

The shadows of dementia are deep—very deep, indeed. They darken our idea of self, which is the very core of our existence. The idea of self provides the reference point that makes our perception of the world understandable. It defines the reach and relevance of our consciousness. It informs us of where, and when, we are in space and time; it tells us what we are, and it tells us what we are not. Progressive dementia relentlessly erodes the brain and inevitably diminishes the brain areas which enable that central concept of self, which includes the positioning of the self in space and time.

These perceptions sometimes eventually vanish altogether in the late stages of dementia, and it is at that point, it seems to me, that the afflicted individual loses her *life*; the physical death of the body becomes just a merciful release from her sufferings in the end. For when the idea of self disappears, the victim is set adrift in a world of absolute strangers, divorced from time and space. And that world of strangers includes herself, whom she no longer recognizes as such. She has no idea of where, or what, she is. It must be a terrifying world. I sensed my Claire's entry into it; I could feel her terror. My knowledge (or more accurately, sensing) of it acutely deepened my feelings of helplessness. I knew that there was absolutely no return, no escape, from that fearsome realm, except death.

This has been a thoroughly dismal analysis of dementia, but dementia is, of course, quintessentially dismal. I ask myself, often, why I pursue the subject. What is the answer? It is not a simple obsession. Claire was epileptic; she suffered seizures that profoundly, if momentarily, altered and disrupted the totality of her cognition. And so the subject of cognition, the understanding of it, fascinated her.

It had fascinated me, too, even before I had entered university. I don't remember exactly what the inspiration was, but my fascination led me to become a philosophy major. My experience as such was not always satisfying. The analyses of cognition at that time were clever and often absorbing, but they were not often supported by scientific findings. This was in the 1950s, before modern neuroscience was even a dream.

Neuroscience has emerged and really blossomed in the last twenty years or so. Even though it's still in its early stages, it has cast a brilliant light on a multitude of brain functions. Much to my delight, Claire was able to understand a lot of it before she descended into the final stages of her dementia. Neuroscience will continue to make astounding progress—the momentum is irresistible—and in the process it will explicate and illuminate epilepsy and dementia and suggest remedies for them, hopefully rendering those afflictions extinct within a few generations.

That is why I am forever thinking and writing about neurological pathologies. They devastated our lives, Claire's and mine, but the swift and brilliant progress of neuroscience fills me with hope for the future. A human life lasts for only an instant in this fleeting world, but it's a wonderful instant, full of light and color and imagination thanks to the miraculous brains we have evolved as humans. These brains deserve to be studied, understood, and cared for to the fullest extent of our capabilities.

Postscript:

Going Home, The Last Journey

I whispered from the shadows
hoping to keep you,
but you slid past my soft words
with a sad smile
and a little sigh,
never stopping,
impatient to embrace
that final journey, that going home,
that last sweet hospice of your soul.

"Going home" is perhaps the fondest wish of most dementia victims, and it is often voiced. "Home" is a vague idea for them; it can mean a return to early childhood or to happier years, or just somewhere, anywhere, other than where they find themselves. It is usually their destination when they wander off. The final "going home" is really the final act in the tragedy of dementia. I have attempted to convey that feeling in the little poem above, which I wrote in June 2012, on the second anniversary of Claire's death.

But it is not the final act for us, the caregivers. We must

begin again, looking forward instead of back, cherishing the past but not trying to relive it. We must take care of ourselves from now on, and we must encourage others who are living in the nightmare from which we have just awakened. We are the survivors; we know exactly what they are going through—no one else really does—and we have the power to help ease their pain. We must never pass up an opportunity to do so.

PART II

Claire at the age of seven, 1941

Claire's college graduation portrait, 1956

Our wedding in San Francisco, 1961

In Hawaii, about 1975

At our farm on the island of Hawaii. Claire had been
a great teacher - she loved children, and children
always responded enthusiastically to her.

At our home in Arizona, 1992

Claire loved to do colored pencil drawings of old
houses—this is a black and white version of the original.

Claire and Me:

An Emotional Journey

We shared a world of warmth and light,
still shining through the veil of night.

This is a sort of diary of my thoughts and feelings, joyful and sad, about our extremely close marriage. Both of us were only children—we were born in the middle of the Great Depression, and our parents could not afford to have more. We were a pair of scrawny kids in our twenties when we met, and we instantly clicked together into a unit as though we had been specifically designed to do so. We were always just plain comfortable with each other, and to me that is the very foundation of a nice marriage; ours was exceptionally nice, and it lasted for almost fifty years. My sadness at the eventual loss of my funny friend can never overwhelm the joy of that marriage, and her death has not put the slightest dent in my love. These thoughts and poems, written over a period of almost three years, have eased my passage into the radically transformed life I live today. Let me say again that the very act of writing them down has helped me to survive that passage, and I hope with all my heart that they may help all of you who are forced to walk this same sad path.

Seasons

After a visit to Claire's hometown, August 2010

In the spring, the early spring,
we would often greet our mornings with a smile
and share the wonders of our dreams.
Oh, such dreams, shining in the morning sun
like our small white dogs, on their morning run;
how shining white, those smiling dreams,
how bright, those wondrous dreams of spring,
and what wondrous hopes they did bring.

Sometimes, in the summer
—warm summer, especially near its end,
when autumn's soft, sweet sadness
can just be sensed around the bend—
we would sit and watch the sunset,
right at dusk, when the setting sun
had set the clouds afire in the west
and sent long shadows across the land:
long, dark shadows across our land.

When autumn set in with gentle glow,
its rich soft light enchanting every space
and warming every tree in colorful embrace,
we would speak in soft tones of our love,

of love that shone like colored leaves,
of love that sweetly conquered all;
but then there came the winds of fall,
the subtle, gentle winds of fall.

Are there only shadows in this winter of our life?
Shadows, and the soft echo of some sweet song,
its words forever lost in time,
and perhaps a whisper of her voice, or mine;
or are there bits of those bright dreams,
still fresh and white, still shining in the morning light,
still shimmering in the shadows, barely seen?

My Little Ghost

On the occasion of our forty-ninth anniversary,
Thanksgiving Day 2010

Come on out, my wee, shy ghost; please come and talk to me.
I saw the flash of your green eyes in the shadow of that tree;
I saw the hem of your bright dress, and the angle of your knee.
We'll sit and chat, all close and warm, just like we used to be,
then if you tell me you can't stay, I must surely set you free,
and we'll wait for that sweet time when I can go home with thee.

Anniversary

*On the occasion of our fiftieth
anniversary, November 23, 2011*

It was the springtime of our life,
that autumn day; the morning breeze
had paved the streets with tawny leaves
and ushered in a shining swirl of mist,
a sweet setting for our timeless tryst:
two lives now fashioned into one
until the end of time should come.

Fifty years of love and joy!
But "love and joy"
does seem such a feeble phrase
to circumscribe those shining days
when we had shared a world of light
now darkened by the veil of night;
darkened,
yet forever bright.

This Fleeting World:

Shadows

After the Diamond Sutra

Thus shall you think of all this fleeting world:
A star at dawn, a bubble in a stream,
A flash of lightning in a summer cloud,
A flickering lamp, a phantom, and a dream.

Foundations

Summer 2010

This was written after Claire had died, a couple of days after I had run across, and read, the letters we had written to each other in the course of the summer of 1961. We had met in early June of that year, just after she had finished her school year as a first-grade teacher and I my first-year law school finals. Our blind date had been arranged by a law-school classmate of mine who had been dating her roommate. The three of them drove up from the peninsula and picked me up in San Francisco, and we toured some of the wineries around Saint Helena. During the course of that tour I became thoroughly smitten. When we returned to San Francisco, my classmate and his date dropped us off. We picked up my car and went out to dinner, after which I took Claire back to her apartment in Palo Alto. She slyly left her gloves in my car when I dropped her off, and I slyly pretended not to notice, which gave me the excuse to call her the next day and offer to return the gloves, which led to dinner and an all-night conversation.

We weren't apart very much after that until we both departed the Bay Area later in June to spend the summer with our parents: she in Prescott, Arizona, and I in Honolulu. Our parents must have been bewildered by the sheer number of letters their kids, who had never been enthusiastic correspondents, were writing and receiving. I think we both told our mothers, who became very curious, that we'd "met someone," but the situation didn't become clear to any of them until we announced our marriage plans in September.

This poem sounds sad, but I was actually exhilarated by the experience of reading those letters. I had been reluctant to do so because I'd thought they might make me sad, but the experience reminded me of the nice start to the really tremendous life we had had together before Claire's dementia became unmanageable. The dementia had partially erased my memories of all the joys of that life, and reading the letters brought a lot of those memories back.

Pathways

We have wandered joyously, just we two,
amongst the rolling hills, roaming through
the tangled pathways of our space and time;
we have overwhelmed the promises
of those halting, passionate letters, full of truth,
which filled the last lonesome summer of our youth
—oh, how our parents must have wondered!
We have shared the comfort of a smile, of a gentle touch,
of words of warmth and kindly grace and, just as much,
of perfect times of silence, enjoying perfect peace.
Tell me, my sweet love; oh, please tell me how—
how shall I bear these lonesome summers now?

Claire

Spring 2010

The progressive dementia that took Claire's life in the end was devastating, but there were flashes of compassion and intelligence even during its final stages. I know that I have covered this subject in the first part of this book, but I find it so remarkable that I am compelled to mention it again. A final flash of rationality is not uncommon in dementia cases, and to me it is of utmost significance. I believe that it is a manifestation of the ultimate resilience, and the triumph, of a fundamental drive toward compassion and love, the drive that makes us so especially human. And I do believe that this drive is possessed in a similar form by other animals—dogs, for instance—and who knows, maybe even other creatures, like little birds. When Claire told me that she needed professional help and that I should take good care of myself when she had gone, she had less than four months left before her dementia took her life. Shortly after our conversation she reverted to her demented state, but my gentle friend retained the heart of her loving and compassionate soul until the very end, and I can feel its presence even now. This poem is about that.

Rustling Leaves

I thought I saw a flash of light, just at dawn,
in the garden where she loved to work and stroll,
before the fog crept in, so long ago.
Was that a ghost, that fleeting form?
It would have been a gentle ghost; she was always so,
and always kind, and quick to smile, and warm.
I called her name, "Claire."
There had been a gentle breeze, rustling the leaves,
but now the leaves were still, and she was gone.

Places and Spaces and Time
Spring 2010

There is no reference point when one of the parties in a long and loving relationship is afflicted with progressive dementia. Reality has been altered forever; one just knows that there is no "where" in space and therefore no "when" in time anymore. In the course of trying to remember things, the caregiver is sometimes struck with the idea that time is something that unrolls—an ethereal something but a substance nonetheless—upon which is imprinted forever all that has ever occurred in the universe. Our whole lives are there, and if we were somehow able to loop back into it, we would meet ourselves coming around a bend. It is a weird feeling, and it intensifies after the demented partner has died and the caregiver is left trying to make some sense out of what has happened to him. Memories of his longtime partner before the onset of dementia are vital to that effort, and those memories of her begin to spring from that loop in the ethereal reality of time. But, of course, there's a catch; we can never quite get back into that loop, and so the memories are fuzzy and indistinct. The details are blurred, the time frame is uncertain, and the "when" and the "where" still elude our understanding. Thus this little poem.

Where have we been for all this past year?
We have been everywhere, but we haven't been here;
we haven't been here, my love, and we haven't been there.
Just yesterday I asked, Please, may I brush your hair?
May I brush your hair, my love? but you weren't there;
I looked everywhere, but we weren't anywhere.
How shall I care for you if we're never here?
Where have we been for all this past year?

The Solace of Uncertainty

We sense time as instantaneous, but because of the way the universe and our brains are structured, our perception of the present moment is not instantaneous. First, it takes time for the light and sound emanating from objects within the range of our senses to reach us; the speeds of light and of sound are fast, but finite, in this universe. And second, much more significantly, it takes time, real time, for our brains to translate and process our sensations—the signals produced by our sense organs—into perceptions. Thus, we are always living in a fleeting "now" moment in time, always speeding forward into the future. But we are already in the future when we perceive that moment, which by then has already become the past.

How can we be certain of anything? Just where does reality end and illusion begin? Evolution has produced a speedy brain—capable of dealing with the flux that is reality—in its relentless progress toward improved survival, but it can never produce a brain that works instantaneously. Nonetheless, evolution and other forces are relentlessly pushing us and the entire universe toward greater complexity and order, never mind the second law of thermodynamics. Can we thereby posit a "teleology," a purpose, in nature? It's tempting but maybe a little premature, even though many mainstream scientists and philosophers are currently seriously considering it. Is this little discussion at all significant? Only, perhaps, in relation to the two poems that follow. They connect my feelings of loss with the realities of time and of substance, of dreams and of possibilities, of the eclipse of individual death in the radiant idea of cosmic evolution. All these ideas soothe me with the strange solace of uncertainty, over which the raven has no more control than I. Of that, at least, I am certain.

Shapes and Shadows

Winter 2011–2012

There had been dark trumpets of despair
sounding down the tunnels of the wind,
then the haunting whisper of a violin
gliding sweetly through the evening air,
bringing memories, stark and spare,
into shaky focus;
but now there's just that bell,
only the one,
singing clearly, sharply, in the night,
filling all my darkened corners with its light.

Why are we here?
But we are not here, nor there,
neither when, nor where;
the instant flash of fleeting time
like the blinking cursor that caps this line
measures out our time in space
and forms the shape and substance of our race
racing across time's razor edge,
at once then and now and yet to appear.

Can we ever sense sweet nature's will?
Perhaps not,
but now it's quiet, warm and still;
the sunshine falls in golden droplets on the hill
where my love lies sleeping, all is well:
her journey done,
her spirit rests serenely in that bell,
just the one,
singing kindly, gently, day and night,
lifting up my darkened spirits with her light.

Quoth the raven, "nevermore."
But I'm not afraid of you, Mr. Raven,
not any more,
I've got your number;
just remember.

An individual life has form in all dimensions. It has depth and breadth; it soars at times to great heights, and when death comes a well-filled life is rounded out in time—completed, not finished, because nothing that has been can be nullified. It remains an essential part of that tapestry that is being woven in the warp and woof of space and time.

—Louise B. Young

I have often been asked whether I believe in life after death, and I always demur; I'm just not certain, even though I am somewhat inclined to think that it's a possibility. My ideas of what its form and substance might be have been deeply influenced by the writings of the physicist Louise Young, who passed away at the age of 92 just last year. Her philosophy is very much in line with the Gaia theory, developed by the chemist James Lovelock and the biologist Lynn Margulis in the 1980s, which posits that the earth and, perhaps, the entire universe are living systems, with their extensions in space and time, and as such they have been constantly evolving in the direction of order and complexity since the beginnings of their existence. And our human lives are, of course, small parts of the biosphere and of the universe itself. Young's assertion that "nothing that has been can be nullified" resonates with me, and that idea is what encouraged me to write this optimistic little poem.

The Tunnels of the Wind

March 2012

You made our lives a lovely dream,
my ever kind and gentle friend;
I know one day you'll come for me
and softly take me by the hand,
and I will gladly go with thee
dancing down the tunnels of the wind.

She loved music, did my Claire, and drama, and poetry, and painting. She loved Brahms and Beethoven, Shakespeare and Frost, and the wonderful, shining paintings of J. M. W. Turner. She would have been deeply moved by the music of Henryk Gorecki; I don't think she ever heard any of it, but I thought of her the other night when his masterpiece was aired on our classical station. Gorecki was a Pole; he composed the *Symphony of Sorrowful Songs* to commemorate the triumph of the human spirit in the face of the incredible horrors of the Holocaust and other Nazi endeavors. He has overwhelmed the horror of those endeavors with the beauty of his music.

Music

After hearing Henryk Gorecki's SYMPHONY OF SORROWFUL
SONGS *with soprano Dawn Upshaw, spring 2012*

Musicians are sculptors of the air;
with their music, dark or fair,
they cut as boldly as they dare
to shape great beauty from despair.

She does not weep; instead, she sings,
and sorrow flees on golden wings.

The Final Decision

Written a few days after her death in June 2010

I have been writing, in a desultory manner, a paper about the totality of the dementia experience that Claire and I had to deal with, at first together and then individually, after she had been overwhelmed by it. This took place over a period of about eight years. I began the paper with the little poem I have reproduced here, which is really about the ending, the wrenching experience of that inevitable last decision. The final six months of her life seemed to last forever, in the form of a slow and agonizing species of nightmare from which no one who has experienced it ever fully awakens. Reality just disappears; it vanishes without a trace.

The ultimate decision—that awesome and awful decision of life or death—devolved, of course, onto me. I thought that I had been sucked dry of emotion by that final nightmare, but unfortunately I had not. In the course of the last four or five days of its duration she had descended into a vegetative state, her brain barely able to keep her essential bodily functions going. The hospice doctor told me that any continued life support would be worse than futile; it would only prolong her agony and mine. Those facts had become obvious to me several days before, but my awareness of them did nothing to assuage my grief. It was not an unanticipated decision; we had fortunately often discussed such things. I did not hesitate to make it, nor would she have questioned it; but it was brutal. Brutal—but it is simple, this final decision. Just like the sunset cloud, it is complex at a certain level, but its complexities are evanescent, as are all things in this fleeting world. They become irrelevant and they evaporate when they are examined in the bright light of eternity. The process is clearly impossible to describe, and when it's happening to you it seems impossible to survive; but here I am. *Mirabile dictu.*

> Such a day I had never before been through,
> but I did act as though I knew, as though I knew;
> I did do this and that, and I did think thus and so,
> I did remember, too, your yearning to go home.
> What was it you said before you left to roam?
> What was it we had thought, what did I need to know?
> Would you have told me: It's not so simple? Would you
>   tell me so?
> Ah, but it is;
> it's as simple as a sunset cloud, with its evanescent glow.

Sundowning

Claire was always very thoughtful; I was often surprised at the depth and clarity of her perceptions. But toward the end she became especially pensive at the close of day, just as it was getting dark, and that pensiveness slowly evolved into the night terror of dementia. I recall often the pain I felt because I had lost the power to bring her back.

Windows of the Night

*Late May, 2012, as I neared the fifty-first anniversary of
our meeting and the second anniversary of her death*

What do you see at the end of day,
staring through the windows of the night
searching for the ghost of your sweet soul?
Oh, please, do quickly tear yourself away
lest you slip into some shadowed hole
whence no one can ever make you whole;
there's no safe return to the realm of light
from those darkling caverns of the night.

The passing of a loved one—especially of one's life partner,
and especially after having dealt with her inexorable decline
into dementia—leaves the survivor dazed and disoriented,
wondering about the meaning of life. There are times when
life itself seems insignificant, even threatening. The memory
of the wonderful life and love we shared soon banishes those
thoughts for me, but they still sometimes creep in unbidden,
mostly around the edges of the saddest of our anniversaries.

Remnants

The second anniversary of her death, June 2012

Fine praise and pleasant flattery,
fleeting fame and passing fancies,
the glowing beauty of our youth:
we drag remnants of ourselves
along behind us for a while;
no one knows, no one cares
but we, we care:
ever selfish, hugging tight
our brightly colored trinkets,
gossamer mementos of our lives.

Dementia:

the Silence

The third anniversary of her entry into the care facility, April 2013

Leaving the home
where beloved ones are sent
to while their silent days away,
I passed a man, perhaps as old as I,
seated on a bench along the hall,
along the path to my escape.

At my glance, he fell in upon himself,
And hiding in the shadow
of the sparse remnants of his existence,
he curled up tight, like a sleeping cat,
and looked away.

So
how fast can you run, old man?
Which way is that exit now?
How can you escape?
Silence, like a stalking cat,
pursues us all with mindless grace,
pursues us all the while
until we tire; then it smiles.

This Fleeting World:

Comfort and Love

I know that true love needs no words,
but what is love to little birds?
Well, I met one once, a perky wren
who brought me back to life again
when I thought I'd like to die:
I'd gone walking, morose and blue
and lo, she landed on my shoe,
then, just before she flew,
she cocked her head and looked me in the eye,
just like my Claire was wont to do;
I smiled, and with a chirp, she was on her way,
and I lived to love another day

What is spirituality? It is perhaps best described as deep emotional involvement with all of existence or, to put it in another way, the full awareness of the self as an integral part of the universe. It can take the form of a religious conviction: worship and love of a god, a reality greater than our own, existing above or beyond the universe but somehow connected with it.

It can also take the form of a non-religious universal love, without a belief in any supernatural reality, a love inspired by the realization that we are all parts of a dynamic, living universe and therefore of everything in it. This is an idea central to the system of thought that is Buddhism, which holds that the self is illusory and fleeting and must be abandoned. But I think that what is really meant by this "negation of the self" is that the individual "self" is redefined as being an inseparable part of the totality of the universe. And that is what I consider to be the explanation for my encounter with that little bird.

It happened at the very peak of my worst care-giving time, Claire's dementia was fast becoming impossible for me to deal with, and I felt terrible because I was thinking of taking her to a memory-care facility. I wasn't really suicidal; I loved her too much to leave her like that, but I had been wrestling with that idea just before the wren made her landing. She was completely unafraid. She looked me straight in the eye, and she gave me a thoroughly happy chirp when she left, quite unhurriedly. She had come to reassure me, and when I smiled she knew that she had succeeded. Crazy? I don't think so.

Identity Theft

While we are on the subject of the self, let's think about self-image, which emerges as the end product of the efforts of our brains to put together our perceptions from the fleeting glimpses we get of ourselves. These are mostly caught out of the corners of our eyes, and all are viewed from inside our own heads. In addition, most of us are at least occasionally somewhat introspective, looking inward and trying to figure out who we are. Once in a while we even incorporate the opinions of friends and acquaintances into our cogitations too, but we seldom take these opinions at face value. We do, nonetheless, in the end come up with a general idea of who and what we are: of our identity, an entirely subjective idea, because we have no way of really stepping out of ourselves and having an unbiased look. And we are constantly changing. Throughout our long marriage, Claire and I would sometimes wonder out loud just what we might have been like twenty years before, but we always came to the same conclusion as I do now, when I look into the mirror whilst shaving and see a strange, scrawny old man peering back at me:

Solitaire

Summer 2012

Oh, strange little old man,
what are you thinking now?
You peer at me with furrowed brow
from the dim recesses of my memory.
You think you can remember me
just as I was, long ago;
but no,
—and neither can I,
so swallow that sigh.

(Has anyone figured out how to shave without looking
into a mirror? Let me know.)

This Fleeting World:
Life and Music

Claire introduced me to her native Arizona soon after we were married, and I have always loved it as much as she did. After our twenty-year sojourn in my native Hawaii, we moved here, and we soon came to appreciate the benefits of our decision. There is a cultural dynamism in Phoenix: art and music are everywhere. Some of it is pretty avant-garde, but not just for show—most of it is sophisticated rather than merely bizarre. One of the prime cultural assets of the region has been the Phoenix Chorale, which has been in existence since 1958. The group lately teamed up with the young Norwegian composer Ola Gjeilo, as their composer in residence in 2009–10, to produce a stunning recording entitled *Northern Lights*.

Northern Lights
July 2012

A soft whisper
becomes a swelling harmony,
sweet voices melting into one.
Life is love;
love is music,
pure and clean and bright,
reaching back to the birth of time
and racing into eternity
on a brilliant beam of light.

Gettysburg Revisited

Claire and I visited Gettysburg some twenty years ago, and when I had occasion to fly to the Baltimore area last year, I felt somehow compelled to see the battlefield again. It is set in the beautiful rolling hills of southern Pennsylvania. I settled in to a pleasant hotel not far from the scene of all the turmoil that had taken place almost a hundred and fifty years before, and the next day I toured the battlefield. The spirit of the place engulfed me this time. The setting is so beautiful and calm that it is hard to imagine such a fierce and hateful battle could ever have raged through it. But after the sun sets, the darkness transforms it, and it becomes serenely mystical. All of existence seems to snap into focus, and hints of the answers to the profoundest of life's questions begin to emerge from the fog of history.

Battlefield Gettysburg

October 2011

Day is done, the field is still, the strident guides gone home;
we who roamed that field in wonder, together but alone,
have returned in thoughtful silence to our rooms.
All is dark,
yet I can see the outline of the trees,
and there's a whisper of a breeze
dancing through the resting park.

Here she is, a wisp, a whisper of a breeze,
whisking her fingers gently down the screen
outside my window, as if to tease.
That's what my love would have done,
if she were here; but there is no one,
just a playful little breeze, unseen.

A whisper, a gentle breath
skipping across that awful field,
which once suffered surfeit of death,
now quiet, peaceful, and benign,
resting in the dark, without a sign
of its olden tragic yield.
Tell me, my little breeze,
why do we come here, you and I,
and all the world; can you say why?

Quiet, a quiet breeze,
barely ruffling the solemn night,
such a night:
so full of meaning, sad and dark,
alive with secrets of that fatal park.
But do I hear a murmur of sweet song?
A peaceful sound, so clear and bright,
to drive away the shadows of the night?
Is that our breeze?
Perhaps she is the spirit of this place,
this serenely sacred place
at once dreadful and replete with grace,
singing just for our hearts' ease;
our gentle breeze,
singing softly in the dark

Perhaps

November 2012

Perhaps there *are* ghosts, in the form of memories and of dreams that bring them to life.

I thought I heard your voice last night,
your gentle voice, so soft and bright,
and then I felt your touch, feathery light,
just as I closed my eyes and fell
into the warm embrace of eternity,
or so it seemed,
perhaps to dream;
but I could tell
that you were there beside me.

Our little dog, the one who loved you most,
had followed you to bed,
and with a happy yawn
had curled up snugly by your side;
she always kept you safe and warm.

But how could this be? All seemed well
in our sweet dream,
yet the two of you had long been gone;

would you vanish with the dawn?
I somehow knew that you would not;
it seemed you two
had reclaimed the spot
deep in my heart
that I keep reserved for you,
never more to part—
perhaps.

Our fifty-first anniversary reminded me of Louise Young's idea of our universe as a work in progress. We are, all of us, a part of that universe, and we will be so for all eternity, for "nothing that has been can be nullified."

The Comfort Zone

November 2012

Beginnings, often happenstance:
a casual meeting, a shy smile
returned, a fond embrace, romance,
two lives melt into one, and all the while
sweet music, the rhythm of a lifelong dance.

The middle years, the comfort zone;
the center shifts from "I" to "we";
we will never be again alone,
bound by love but forever free.

Death, the ending, sad yet foreseen;
but love is power, unscathed by death,
and nothing can destroy the dream
we lived full well with every breath.

Love, the weaver of the universe,
unites all things that seem diverse:
out of many she shapes the whole;
she has always been sweet nature's soul.

In the End

February 5, 2012

Earlier this year I was looking out the window of an airplane as I was waiting to take off for Hawaii, where Claire and I had spent a good deal of our married life. Just then a gust of wind blew some brown leaves into the air, which reminded me of the ultimate evanescence of this world. I was moved to write this on the back of my boarding pass.

Reflections

Memories:
Little drifting bits of dreams
fluttering in the winter air.
What have we else?

What have we else? But then, what else do we need? We have the universe.

Through the Gates

December 27, 2012

This morning, standing at the window,
I watched the full moon slide
behind the dark mountains to the west;
the gates of the universe
you often called them
when we stood at that window,
close and warm, side by side,
riding the moon on its bright glide
through those shadowed gates,
into the vast and shining reaches of eternity.

CPSIA information can be obtained at www.ICGtesting.com
Printed in the USA
BVOW05s0246290814

364706BV00001B/1/P